Upton House and Gardens

WARWICKSHIRE

A souvenir guide

National Trust

THE COUNTRY HOUSE WEEKEND IN THE 1930s

Why, in a period when the productive value of land was negligible, did wealthy people want to own country houses? The life of the Samuel family at Upton in the 1930s provides some answers to the question.

Upton House belonged in the 1930s to one of the richest men in Britain, Walter Samuel, 2nd Lord Bearsted (1885–1948). His father had founded Shell, and the growth of the oil industry after 1900 interlocked with the family's shipping and banking activities. His parents owned a large house near Maidstone, but in 1919 Walter Samuel bought Sunrising House near Upton and enlarged it considerably as a base for hunting. When Upton House came on the market in 1927, he seized the opportunity of improving an historic but rather ramshackle estate, as well as strengthening its original architectural character.

Prestige and pleasure
The prestige conferred by owning a country house was originally linked to the political power of land ownership, so that, even today, some might consider it odd if someone with the financial means to afford a 'country place' does not acquire one. Coupled to that, however, is a much stronger underlying ideal of lifestyle. Since ancient Rome, poets and moralists have preferred the country to the town. It offers health, peace, a reminder of the cycle of the seasons, and the opportunity to re-engage with nature through gardening, farming and field sports. It is a place of entertainment, offering these pleasures to those lacking them in town. The country is usually seen as the proper place for children to grow up and achieve independence away from the moral hazards of the city.

The long weekend
In the age of mass transport, the weekend became the counterpart of the working week, a longed-for escape and change of gear, to be experienced intensely, because it was so brief. In 1940, a history of the 1930s by Robert Graves used the title *The Long Week-End* to characterise the whole period. For those who worked in the country, even the modest country house became the centre of a local micro-economy, providing direct and indirect employment and dispensing benefits in its sphere of influence.

Below Walter Samuel, 2nd Viscount Bearsted, who lived at Upton in the 1930s and created the house we see today

Right Dorothea, Lady Bearsted

> 'At a weekend party, guests would arrive on Friday, in time for dinner, there would be hunting in season on Saturday, golf and other sports on Sunday before leaving Sunday evening or Monday morning.'
>
> Albert Beck, second footman

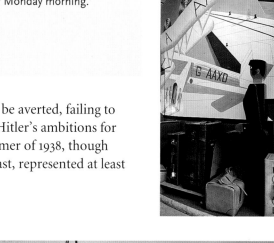

3

The lifestyle of the 2nd Viscount Bearsted was not ostentatious. He and his family conformed to the evolving conventions of the time, which were simpler than before the First World War, but which still demanded special clothes for different activities and times of day – the formality of dining, the importance of hunting – and meticulous attention to the visual presentation of the house and garden.

1938: An illusion of peace

1938 was a year in which people in Britain were becoming increasingly aware of the threat of another war, even though Prime Minister Neville Chamberlain thought that he had ensured 'peace in our time' in the Munich Agreement with Adolf Hitler. The previous two years had seen the turbulence of the Abdication Crisis, followed by the coronation of King George VI. British people were encouraged to believe in continuity and the values of home and family, and the British Pavilion at the Paris International Exhibition that year depicted a country of leather luggage, tennis, country crafts and simple rural pleasures, based around the idea of the weekend away from town. By 1939, many still hoped that war could be averted, failing to see the fanaticism of Hitler's ambitions for Germany, so the summer of 1938, though metaphorically overcast, represented at least an illusion of peace.

Top right The British Pavilion at the 1937 Paris International Exhibition

Above Lady Bearsted's Bedroom in the 1930s

REMODELLING THE HOUSE AND GARDENS

The early history of Upton House is described on pp.50–1.

The atmosphere of the interiors, and much of the shape of the exterior and garden, is owed to the remodelling carried out in 1927–8 by the 2nd Lord Bearsted. He chose the architect Percy Morley Horder (1870–1944), whose designs included the original University of Nottingham, several Congregational churches and a Cambridge college, as well as numerous houses and alterations, many locally in the Cotswolds.

Below The entrance front after remodelling; photographed in 1931

Quality without ostentation

About 40 per cent of Upton House consists of 20th-century fabric, added at each end of the original central rectangle, which had already been extended over time. Externally, the new work tactfully enhanced the character of the earliest features and maintains the gorgeous warmth of the local iron-rich Hornton stone. The long horizontals, combined with the axial formality of the approach and forecourt, bring out the French quality of the original building. Internally, however, every room is a new creation, with details based on 17th-century design, but regularised and reinterpreted in the same spirit one associates with the clipped accents and streamlined fashions of the period. James Lees-Milne, visiting for the National Trust in 1946, found 'nothing of consequence architecturally save a few beautiful 18th-century chimneypieces and a beautiful Coleshill-style staircase, rearranged by Lord B. and extended'. With hindsight, it is possible to take a more positive view. Everything is of the best quality, without excess or ostentation, apart, perhaps,

An architect of temperament

'Horder possessed the artistic temperament in excess: he cultivated a bohemian appearance, and exasperated his clients and contractors by his erratic, wayward, and unbusinesslike habits; in his office his pupils nicknamed him "Holy Murder".'

Dictionary of National Biography

from the film star quality of the main bathroom. The paint colours, chosen mainly by Lady Bearsted, are similarly uniform, with a dominant colour in each room, reflecting a 1920s taste for textured effects that was popularised by Basil Ionides, the designer of the new Savoy Theatre in 1929 and husband of Lord Bearsted's sister, Nellie. The cartoonist and architectural humorist Osbert Lancaster described this style, which was popular among art collectors, as 'Curzon Street Baroque', and Upton is a precious survival. The 'Knole sofa', held together by tasselled cords, is its trademark.

Making the garden

Morley Horder's work in the garden includes the plain stone features of the main terrace and the intimate west terrace leading easily out of the newly created sports room. Lady Bearsted's garden designer, Kitty Lloyd Jones, collaborated with a local mason to create the dramatic flight of steps linking the garden terraces, using rough drystone walling, with careful attention to the size of the steps and the paving patterns

Below Upton is a rare surviving example of 'Curzon Street Baroque', as the cartoonist Osbert Lancaster christened this fashionable 1930s style

underfoot. This formal garden architecture offers a matrix around which less formal planting can develop. At the roadside, Horder designed typical 17th-century gate-piers and Baroque ironwork with a French-style *clairvoyée* ('opening') in the form of side railings and stone curbs 'intended to contain strong planting'.

The desire to recreate the imagined atmosphere of the 18th century was a relatively novel feature of taste even in the 1920s, but one that became universal from the royal family downwards and was equally popular in the USA, producing its own distinctive variation on the original theme. At Upton it binds together the house and its contents.

Above Kitty Lloyd Jones designed the stone stairs that link the garden terraces
Below The Knole sofa in the Picture Gallery

LIVING AT UPTON

The 2nd Lord Bearsted owned four houses in total. His London house (a Crown lease) was No.1 Carlton Gardens (close to Parliament and the London clubs), which he gave to the nation as the official residence of the Foreign Secretary in 1939. He also owned Phones House, near Aviemore, as a shooting lodge, and a house, larger than Upton, at Cap Ferrat on the French Riviera. Most men of means would aspire to divide their time in a similar way: London for the business week; the Riviera for long winter and spring breaks; Scotland for grouse shooting after 12 August; and an English house whose location satisfied Lady Bearsted's passions for hunting and gardening, while allowing Lord Bearsted to show the best items from his art collection in a setting more like a museum than a home.

Above Lady Bearsted was a passionate huntswoman

Below The Inglenook

Upton is in the country of the Warwickshire Hunt. The long straight avenue and the forecourt of the house provide an ideal setting for a 'meet', the beginning of the day's hunting when riders and hounds assemble.

The most unusual feature of the remodelling of the house was the suite of rooms at the north end, where the kitchens had been before. The Sports Room, as it was called on the plans, is also a picture gallery, overlooked at the upper level by the Library. At the lower level, modern structural techniques allow for wide openings between the three parts of the space, including a low-ceilinged sitting area (the Inglenook), and a billiard room. Before 1938, the Squash Court was housed in the space now containing the Picture Gallery. These spaces are less formal than the rooms on the main floor.

Modern comforts

Most of our information about life at Upton in the 1930s comes from former servants or their children. They describe a benign and orderly regime, with a focus on comfort. There was a Swiss chef, Mr Decker (as Lord Bearsted liked the best cooking and, unusually, it was he who supervised the kitchens), and a Swiss lady's maid for Lady Bearsted. The alterations carried out by Morley Horder introduced modern comforts, most notably the luxurious bathroom. Although guests would originally have shared bathrooms, there were wash basins in cupboards in all the bedrooms. Bill Smith, the son of the butler during the 1930s, recalled the grand balls held at Upton in the winter, 'All the servants dressed formally with my father wearing a tail coat with black tie.' Dancing took place in the Long Gallery, although it lacked a sprung dance floor.

7

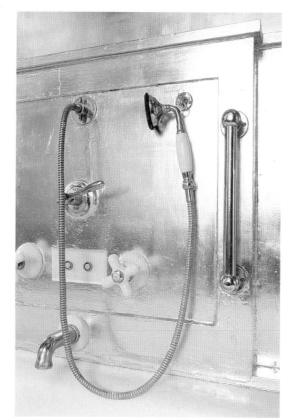

Top *Francis Dukinfield Astley and his Harriers*; by Ben Marshall (No.50; Dining Room)

Above The food at Upton was always of the highest standard

Left Upton was fitted out with the latest mod cons

'CONSEQUENTLY THIS COUNTRY IS AT WAR WITH GERMANY'

Announced Prime Minister Neville Chamberlain at 11.15 a.m. on 3 September 1939 – 15 minutes after the expiration of Britain's ultimatum to Germany to withdraw her troops from Poland.

It would be speculation, of course, but not unreasonable to assume that a man with the 2nd Lord Bearsted's international connections would have believed that war with Hitler's Third Reich was all but inevitable.

Now Upton's house party guests of the previous year could enjoy only recollections of their past way of life – what another house party-goer of the period, Charles Ryder in Evelyn Waugh's Brideshead Revisited, described as *memory, that winged host that soared about me one grey-morning of wartime.*

Throughout the 1930s, Lord Bearsted had worked to facilitate the emigration of Jews from Nazi Germany; and in 1936 he visited America both to raise funds and lobby support for Germany's beleaguered Jewish community.

But from 1938, the Nazis' punitive emigration laws made it increasingly difficult to leave. Nevertheless, in the months running up to the declaration of war, he became involved in the Kindertransport which successfully brought 10,000 Jewish children from Nazi occupied Europe to Britain, where they were placed with foster families.

Above World War 2 Blackout poster

Right Lord and Lady Bearsted moved to the Dorchester Hotel for the duration of the war

Wartime Role

War brought a very different life for the whole family: Lord Bearsted – who'd been awarded a Military Cross in World War 1, now became a Colonel in the Intelligence Corps and worked with the Special Operations Executive (SOE).

Being keen horsemen, his sons Richard (Dick) and Peter fought with the Warwickshire Yeomanry, although once overseas this became an armoured regiment. Tony, however, was excluded from conventional military service due to deafness, though he was accepted by SOE and also went overseas.

The War brought domestic and business changes, too. The Bearsteds' leased London house in Carlton Gardens had earlier been given to the Foreign Secretary, so Lord & Lady Bearsted moved, along with many eminent and famous people, into The Dorchester Hotel – and so vacated Upton for much of the duration.

This enabled the core of the M. Samuel & Co. bank operations - along with twenty-two of its staff - to move immediately upon war's declaration from the East End of London to Upton House, where they remained until the end of the War: the Long Gallery becoming the typing pool, with the bank workers taking their meals here too, surrounded by some of the wonderful art collection.

The unmarried members of staff were put up in the house in guest bedrooms that were specially laid out as single-sex dormitories, while married couples were billeted around the estate. All, though, got to use the swimming pool and had the run of the park, and could explore the surrounding countryside by bicycle. Whilst no doubt concerned about their loved ones in London, the bank workers probably made the most of their stay in the country.

9

Above The male bank workers' dormitory

Left The bank workers of M.Samuel & Co on the steps of the South Terrace at Upton

Above Lord Bearsted (seated) and his 3 sons

Safeguarding the Art

If the staff initially also enjoyed the aesthetic glories of Upton's art collection, this did not last. By late 1941, Lord Bearsted became concerned at the risk of bombing even in the countryside. He approached the very young director of the National Gallery, Kenneth Clark, to ask if he might send some of his collection to join those works from the National Gallery which were then being stored in a disused slate quarry at Blaenau Ffestiniog (Manod) in North Wales.

His request accepted, Lord Bearsted selected forty of the smaller and most special works, including the Bosch triptych, El Greco and the Hogarths. The paintings were duly sent to Wales, where they remained underground until November 1945.

Above Lady Bearsted on her WVS war work

Below Paintings en route to Manod Quarry

Although there were early concerns about nearby falling rocks, conservation conditions in the quarry proved very favourable, and led to advances in understanding in the field of preventative conservation which continue to benefit the collections of the National Trust and others.

The Homecoming

The family and paintings' return to Upton was clearly a cause for great celebration, and the butler's son recalled years later how the house was 'dressed to impress' and that Henry Hall and His Orchestra came down from London for 'the party to end all parties'.

Upton's festivities were short, however, as post-war life proved very different; and within three years both Lord and Lady Bearsted had passed away. Nonetheless, it is a sincere hope that the wish expressed by their second son in in a letter home to his father in 1945 has been fulfilled:

Upton is your beautiful creation
and as such should remain in
beauty and a joy forever.

Opposite *The MacDonald Children* by Henry Raeburn was one of Lord Bearsted's paintings sent to the Manod Quarries.

COLLECTING AND PHILANTHROPY

The National Trust accepted the gift of Upton House on the strength of its collections of paintings and porcelain, acquired by the 2nd Lord Bearsted. His parents were both collectors, and from 1905 onwards he continued adding to their legacy, resulting in a superb collection.

From Old England to Old Masters

Eighteenth-century English portraits were often bought by the new rich at the turn of the century as symbols of social position. Most of those at Upton were acquired by the 1st Lord Bearsted from Lord Romney as part of the contents of The Mote, his country house in Kent, in 1895. The double-height Picture Room added by Morley Horder was apparently built according to an idea of Lady Bearsted to accommodate them.

The 2nd Lord Bearsted made his mark as a picture collector at Christie's in 1928, when he paid a record price of £8,520 for a set of four Francis Wheatleys (no longer at Upton), thus keeping them in Britain. The pictures were exhibited that year at Olympia, and seen as 'a genuine bit of Old England in its eternal freshness and youth'. His collecting was spread over the second half of his life. He identified works as they came on the market, and Sir Alec Martin, a director of Christie's, made bids for him. Bearsted also bought from London dealers, and occasionally, as in the case of *The Death of the Virgin* by Pieter Bruegel the Elder, from another collector with a fortune based on oil, Lord Lee of Fareham. As a Trustee of the National Gallery, Bearsted contributed money towards its acquisitions, and would have had

many opportunities to discuss works on the market with the young Director, Sir Kenneth Clark. As the 1930s progressed, Bearsted's ambitions rose, so that he began to acquire works by major European masters, including the triptych attributed to Hieronymus Bosch in 1937, followed by the Tintoretto and El Greco, along with the pair of Hogarths, the following year. By this point, which coincided with the construction of the new gallery at Upton in place of the former Squash Court, he had surely begun to think of his collection as a potential gift to the nation.

Above George Romney's *William Beckford* was one of the full-length 18th-century portraits acquired by Lord Bearsted's father

Right Lord Bearsted bought two of William Hogarth's famous *Times of the Day* series in 1938

Contemporary Art

While Lord Bearsted was clearly a discerning collector of the art of the past, he also took an active interest in the contemporary art of his time, too. Shell commissioned many important artists of the day to produce the now iconic Shell posters. Furthermore, Lord Bearsted was Chairman of east London's Whitechapel Gallery during the post-War years. The Whitechapel concentrates on contemporary works that are often created in the locality, where it undertakes numerous outreach and educational projects too. While his descendants continue to support the Whitechapel, the National Trust at Upton carry on his work to bring contemporary art, as well as works of the 1930s, to the public by organising exhibitions and appointing artists in residence.

The charm of the conversation-piece

It is in the English collection that we can best see some of Lord Bearsted's own story reflected. His sporting pictures were acquired in the years immediately following his purchase of Upton, together with other 18th-century pieces appropriate to the style of the house. The charming works of Arthur Devis at Upton reflect a popular, if rather exclusive taste of the 1920s, in which one can hardly fail to draw connections between the sparsely furnished rooms and serene landscape backgrounds and the simplified lifestyle of country houses of the same years.

Priceless porcelain

The porcelain collection was mainly formed before the acquisition of Upton. It also represents a typical taste of the time, and a collecting area in which women, including Queen Mary and Lord Bearsted's sister, the Hon. Mrs Nellie Ionides, were very active in the inter-war years. Again, English and European pieces of the 18th century dominate.

Good causes

Lord Bearsted was one of the major philanthropists of his age, in line with the Jewish religious obligation *tzedekah* to give money to unknown recipients. His good causes included the two Jewish maternity hospitals in Hampton Wick and Stoke Newington, as well as his involvement in the Kindertransports that safely brought 10,000 Jewish children to Britain from Germany and Austria.

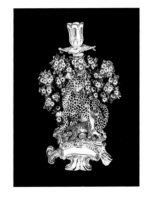

Above A Chelsea porcelain candlestick illustrating Aesop's Fable of the Leopard and the Fox

Left Arthur Devis's *Mr and Mrs Van Harthals and their son* is typical of Lord Bearsted's taste for 18th-century conversation-pieces

TOUR OF THE HOUSE

HALL

The stone-lined Hall creates a formal, even chilly effect for visitors on arrival. This enhances the exterior effect of a small French château rather than an English country house. This effect was introduced as part of Morley Horder's remodelling in 1927–8, when a screen of Doric columns was removed, along with a patterned ceiling. At the same time, the stairs were rebuilt in a different position, so that they come directly down into the Hall. They reminded James Lees-Milne on his 1946 visit of those at Coleshill, a famous 17th-century house in Berkshire, given to the National Trust but destroyed by fire in 1952. The stone chimneypiece, in the manner of William Kent, was already in position.

Hunting

Lady Bearsted, who rode side-saddle in the old-fashioned manner, was passionate about hunting and after 1935 her eldest son, Dick, became joint Master of the Hunt. It is not hard to picture the day of a meet, with a flurry of activity in the hall as family and guests came downstairs in their hunting clothes, to mount their horses in the cold from the mounting blocks flanking the front door. The other members of the hunt, including local farmers and gentry, as well as a few visiting town-dwellers, would have ridden into the courtyard, where the traditional 'stirrup cups' of warming cherry brandy or sloe gin would be handed round. The hounds would be under the control of the huntsmen employed from the Hunt subscriptions to raise and train the pack, along with their kennelman. The Master would sound the 'off' with his hunting horn, and the whole company, led by the hounds, would make their way towards the piece of their 'country' chosen for the day's sport.

Below This 16th- or 17th-century Swiss-German stained-glass panel depicts a hunting scene – appropriate decoration for the Hall

Left The Warwickshire Hunt at the beginning of a day's sport in October 1938

Arriving at Upton

Guests in the 1930s would arrive by car, for which the gravel courtyard allowed a generous turning space. Their luggage would be unloaded by a footman and brought in by the separate door to the left of the front door, to be carried up to their rooms and unpacked by a footman or maid. The architecture and decoration of the entrance hall, with its tapestries and paintings, would have given an immediate impression of good taste, supported by flower arrangements from the garden or hothouses.

LONG GALLERY (currently presented as the Banking Hall)

Morley Horder created the Long Gallery out of three existing rooms within the narrow footprint of the house, creating a magnificent vista, a sort of provincial Versailles. The formal effect is reinforced by the restrained Georgian decoration, the overall use of a single paint colour, and the formal arrangement of furniture on the wooden floor, punctuated by the regular shafts of light from the windows, with their deep reveals. It was originally intended to fill alternate windows with display cases for porcelain, facing the ones on the north wall, but this plan was abandoned because the effect would have been too dark, and, perhaps, more like a museum than a house.

Above The Long Gallery was a place for music, dancing and conversation

The Long Gallery offers comfortable sitting spaces at each end, one being close to the Dining Room, and thus suitable for the ladies to retire to at the end of dinner, while the men remained seated at the table. There is a convenient fireplace tucked into the corner, although the comfort of this large space would depend on central heating. This is the closest that Upton House came to having a drawing room in the more conventional sense, indicating that the family expected to use the Picture Room and its associated spaces for everyday, while the Long Gallery was intended for more formal occasions.

Dutch Old Masters

Among the schools of European art, the Dutch painters were traditionally prized for their skill in observing daily life and landscape, including aspects that contributed to the material prosperity of the Netherlands in the 17th century, such as ships and harbours, and the fruits of trade, including fine objects and food set off by a cool northern light in their houses. Dutch painters also created a style of story-telling picture, often involving comic or grotesque peasants. These trends were assimilated into

English 18th-century paintings, so that the Dutch masters at Upton form a historical background for Lord Bearsted's dominant interest in conversation-pieces and sporting scenes. The flower displays in the paintings would have been mirrored in the actual displays in the Long Gallery. Lord Bearsted had a personal connection with the Netherlands, since his father had been forced in 1906 to sell nearly half the Shell company to Royal Dutch, which had long been both a partner and a rival to Shell, thus creating the multi-national organisation we know today.

Ceramics

Early porcelain has been among collectors' most prized areas of activity for well over a century, supported by its association with royal and princely factories in Europe – led by Meissen in 1708 – when the secret of

Chinese porcelain was rediscovered, and their accomplished and charming imitators in England. The small factories at Chelsea (from 1745), Derby (from 1750), Bow, in East London (from 1746), and Worcester (from 1751) are well represented at Upton. Figures and figure groups predominate, together with pieces that are at least notionally functional as vessels or candlesticks. Typically, these often come in pairs, and were intended for dressing chimneypieces, which offered a prominent but safe place for display in Georgian rooms, where their detail could be seen close up and the modelling would stand out in slanting daylight or candlelight.

The spirit and style of the pieces are predominantly those of the Rococo: a European taste of the mid-18th century that favoured the intimate and feminine, capturing the classical ideal of the enviably simple lives and loves of country people, as seen by those who did not have to endure the hardships of country living. There are also tokens of the exotic worlds of Turkey and the East where British traders were making inroads. Famous men are represented, and the stars of the stage in their favourite roles. In addition, there are fine French pieces from the associated factories of Vincennes and Sèvres, which have always been prized by collectors for their fine bodies and exquisite decoration.

Left *St Catherine's church, Utrecht*; by Pieter Jansz. Saenredam

Above Chelsea figures of Apollo and five of the nine Muses, *c.*1765

Music

In the 1930s, a grand piano stood at the south end of the gallery (where a substitute is seen today) ready, no doubt, for any talented guest to perform at a time when keyboard playing was a polite accomplishment for both sexes, and popular music was in something of a golden age, with the musical comedy songs of Cole Porter, George Gershwin and Noël Coward among the most popular.

SITTING ROOM

The Sitting Room at the end of the Long Gallery is marked on the 1927 plan as 'Boudoir', indicating that it is Lady Bearsted's personal domain on the ground floor, a simple room with a view over the terrace to the hills beyond. It is also close to the equivalent spaces occupied by Lord Bearsted, the Study across the passage, looking out over the entrance courtyard, and the Library, contained in the new wing of the house. The position of these rooms allows for estate staff and other visitors to come on business without going into the main parts of the house.

LIBRARY

The Library is designed in an unusual manner. It is modest in scale, and its connection, via the Balcony, to the Picture Room and family spaces on the lower floor, suggests a perch for supervision of activities below, and for viewing the full-length portraits at eye level. Such expanding spaces, more typical of the Modern Movement in architecture, although still framed in historic details, required ample central heating if they were to avoid the cold draughts otherwise inseparable from open fireplaces. In 1963 the double-height room was floored over to create the proper drawing room missing from the 1927 plan, and a partition separated it from the Library. At that time, a cupboard door was created in one corner, with the traditional device of dummy book spines with jocular references to members of the household, including the book by Higgs, the butler, on his master, and vice-versa, and *Miss Management*, with the initials of the 3rd Lord Bearsted's daughter, Felicity, now the Hon. Mrs Robert Waley-Cohen.

Left The Library with a view into the Picture Room beyond

OPPOSITE
Left *The 1st Earl and Countess of Ely*; by Sir Joshua Reynolds
Right *Crossing the Ford*; by Thomas Gainsborough

Business

As Chairman of Shell Transport and Trading, Lord Bearsted's professional work was undertaken in London, after 1932 in the distinctive office building, Shell-Mex House, overlooking the Thames and designed by Messrs. Joseph – the architects who added the Picture Gallery to Upton House in 1936–8. His London house, 1 Carlton Gardens, was sometimes the scene of special 'Shell' dinners for those most closely connected with the company, but there is no evidence that he brought his work down to Upton when visiting. In the 1930s, the Study would have acted as a place of retreat and suitable for interviews, perhaps with his sons, Dick, Peter and Anthony who, according to a family member who knew them as boys, 'were very idle in their youth', although their father did his best to shape them in his own mould. As the 3rd Viscount, Dick, whose face was badly scarred when his tank was hit while fighting in Italy during the Second World War, had an active career as a director of Hill Samuel (as M. Samuel & Co became) and other City companies. As Chairman of the Whitechapel Art Gallery, in succession to his father, he was responsible for the appointment of Bryan Robertson, one of post-war Britain's most adventurous curators, to the post of Director in 1952, against some opposition from his fellow trustees.

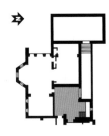

PORCELAIN LOBBY

At the foot of the stairs and added in 1927–9, the Porcelain Lobby contains the best examples from Lord Bearsted's collection of French ceramics. These came from the 2nd Lord Bearsted's London chambers at Albany during the war, and were not installed at Upton until after his death.

Opposite, clockwise from top left A coffee cup and saucer, decorated with a portrait of Benjamin Franklin, who was US ambassador to France in 1776–85. A coffee cup and saucer, 1778, from the service commissioned by Catherine the Great of Russia. A plate made and painted for Madame du Barry, Louis XV's last mistress. She died in 1793, but it was not gilded until after 1795. A *bleu celeste* tray, 1761, decorated with a peasant scene in the manner of David Teniers

Right A *bleu celeste* (sky blue) double jardinière

Sèvres porcelain

Experimental workshops were set up in the royal château of Vincennes south of Paris by 1738–40, and the factory was in regular production by 1745. In 1756 the factory moved to Sèvres, having outgrown its premises. Louis XV bought the factory outright in 1759, having granted the Vincennes factory fourteen years previously the French monopoly on producing porcelain wares with coloured and gilded decoration.

Most of the production at Sèvres was devoted to wares rather than figures. Responsibility for shapes was largely in the hands of Jean-Claude Duplessis, artistic director, 1748–74. He also decided which areas of the pieces should be covered with ground colours. There are six ground colours: *bleu lapis*, a dark blue underglaze ground found on early pieces, after 1751; *bleu nouveau*, a dark blue overglaze ground which replaced *bleu lapis* after 1763; *bleu celeste*, a turquoise ground, derived from imported Chinese wares, first used in 1753; *rose*, a pink ground, after 1757; *vert*, green, first recorded in 1752; yellow, early pieces from 1753 are richer than those of the 1780s and '90s.

Painting in panels reserved on these grounds is a characteristic of much Sèvres porcelain. The choice of subject, as well as other painted decoration, was the responsibility of the second artistic director, Jean-Jacques Bachelier (1748/51–93). Common subjects

were scenes of children after the painter François Boucher, harbour scenes by Morin, while flowers were painted by, among others, Prévost.

The production of Sèvres wares was a time-consuming process. Even the simplest piece in a grand service, such as a plate, passed through the hands of at least eight specialist craftsmen: the moulder, the *répareur*, the glaze painter, the ground artist, the painter of flowers, the painter of cameos, the gilder and the burnisher. And after each major process, except the last, the plate had to be fired. At any stage during this process a piece might be rejected for the slightest imperfection.

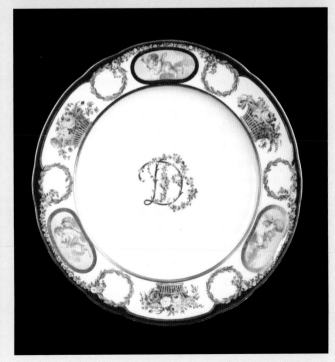

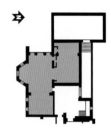

PICTURE ROOM

The Picture Room still contains the full-length portraits collected by the 1st Viscount which it was created to display. The spaces adjoining represent an ingenious way of bringing together a range of activities. Dick Samuel was 20 years old at the time the alterations were completed, and his brothers 18 and 12, so that their parents would already have been aware of the new, less formal behaviour of the younger generation.

Below The double-height Picture Room with the Billiard Room beyond

INGLENOOK

As one enters the Picture Room, the appealing sight of comfortable fireside chairs opens on the left, beneath a low ceiling, where the architectural character suggests an earlier period than the rest of the house, although in fact it dates from Morley Horder's alterations. The space is reminiscent of the later 19th century, when inglenooks, cosy spaces around large hearths suitable for burning logs rather than coal, became symbolic of the heart of the home.

Here, as elsewhere in the house, is a 'Knole' sofa, popular in the inter-war years, with side panels hinged so that, in theory, they can be let down to become a bed. They are fastened to the back by heavily tasselled cords looped over carved wooden posts. The name is taken from a 17th-century example at Knole in Kent (also a National Trust property).

BILLIARD ROOM

The Billiard Room enjoys the gloom appropriate to its evening use. Although television has introduced the world to the more modern game of Snooker, we may assume that the more demanding game of Billiards, involving one red ball and a white cue ball for each of the two contestants, was more frequently played here, as a well-established male occupation for the time between dinner and bed. In the adjacent cupboard, the 3rd Viscount kept an elaborate model railway set, with scenery and buildings mounted on a board designed to fit on the billiard-table.

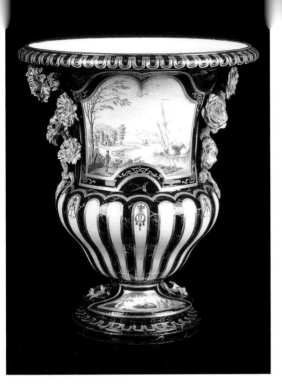

Above *Self-portrait of the Artist Engraving*; by Richard Morton Paye (detail of No.57; Billiard Room)

Left A French Medici vase

Below right An 18th-century Chelsea Pompadour vase

Below *William Weddell, William Palgrave and Weddell's servant, l'Anson*; by Nathaniel Dance, 1765 (No.13; Billiard Room)

PICTURE GALLERY PASSAGE

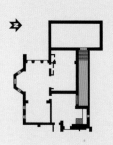

Below *The Duet*; by Gabriel Metsu (No.120)

Below *Le Coup de Soleil*;
by Jacob van Ruisdael (No.126)

Left *Pope Pius VI blessing the People of Venice*;
by Francesco Guardi (No.228)

Below left *Martin Ruzé*; by Franz Pourbus the Younger, 1612 (No.163)
Below *The Disrobing of Christ*; by El Greco (No.255)

PICTURE GALLERY

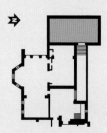

In 1927–36 this area was a squash court, with a gallery that remains visible in the corner. In 1936 it was converted to house Lord Bearsted's growing number of 15th- and 16th-century paintings, which underpin the exceptional quality of the whole Upton collection. The architects, Messrs Joseph, the designers of Shell-Mex House, completed the previous year, followed the best practice of the time in their design of a skylight to provide indirect natural lighting for the pictures. The furniture is chosen to complement the paintings in period and national origin, a practice that was common among collectors in America and Europe. The light fittings are identical to some installed in the National Gallery in the same year.

Below *An Unknown Man*; by Rogier van der Weyden (No.171)

Below *Henri II of France on Horseback*; by François Clouet (No.181)

Right *St Michael slaying the Dragon*; by Jean Fouquet (No.184)

Far right *Two Apostles*; by Carlo Crivelli (No.223)

Below *The Death of the Virgin*; by Pieter Bruegel the Elder (No.148)

The Adoration of the Magi;
attributed to Hieronymus
Bosch (No.143)

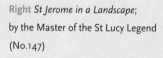

Right *St Jerome in a Landscape*;
by the Master of the St Lucy Legend
(No.147)

Left *The Madonna and Child*;
by Gerard David (No.153)

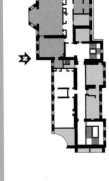

BEDROOM AND BATHROOM

The main bedroom, which was Lady Bearsted's, was furnished in the 1930s with a mixture of 18th-century pieces according to the fashion of the time, including a four-poster bed, a Chinese-style lacquered cabinet and a pair of matching chairs which would have added glitter and colour, although nothing to compete with the adjoining bathroom, where the latest London fashion for the modern French style of decoration, known today as Art Deco, was revealed. Bathrooms of this type, evoking temple-like shrines to health and hygiene, were popular and often illustrated in magazine articles about houses. The *Country Life* writer Arthur Oswald tolerantly accepted it as 'amusing'.

Morley Horder's surviving drawings show a version with a lower vault and green columns, then superseded by the more spectacular red version. The decorative finishes, which went out of fashion after the war, have been painstakingly reconstructed to make this one of the National Trust's star interiors of the 20th century.

Below Lady Bearsted's Bedroom

Below The Chinoiserie red lacquer gramophone in Lady Bearsted's Bedroom

Dressing for dinner

The large numbers of different sets of clothes that Victorian society required a lady of fashion or status to wear in the course of one day had been greatly simplified by the inter-war period. However, the practice of changing for dinner persisted – a pleasant way of marking the end of the day's activities with a pause and a sense of renewal through a bath and fresh clothes, prepared by invisible hands. Gentlemen would wear virtually the same every night, a white tie, piqué dress shirt, low-cut white waistcoat and tailcoat, or, less formally, a black dinner jacket with a black bow tie in the fashion made acceptable at the end of the 1920s by the Prince of Wales (later Edward VIII). These clothes would be laid out by the valet every night in readiness. Ladies would pick from their wardrobe of long dresses, teamed with a short jacket, shawl or wrap against the cold, and shoes to match, with appropriate time spent at the dressing table to ensure that hair and make-up were complete and in order before going downstairs.

Above right The Art Deco Bathroom
Right Morley Horder's design for the Bathroom

DINING ROOM

Before the 1927 alterations, the dining room was in the matching bay addition of 1757 at the west end of the house, where the kitchens were also located, now the upper part of the Picture Room, while this end was used as a billiard room.

The room is mainly notable for the *pictures* that hang in it, including some of Lord Bearsted's best sporting paintings, and the pair of *Haymakers* and *Reapers* by George Stubbs of 1783. The *seat covers* were stitched by the 3rd Lord Bearsted who was encouraged to take up needlework as part of his rehabilitation following injury in the Second World War.

The present paint scheme dates from 1990, replacing a green-brown scheme by the 3rd Lady Bearsted and restoring the 1930s decoration.

Dogs' dinner

The 3rd Lord Bearsted liked to be served steak and kidney pudding here after hunting. On one occasion, he was called away, and on his return found that his dogs had not only seized the dish off the table but successfully dispersed its contents some way up the walls in their enthusiasm.

Above *The Haymakers*; by George Stubbs (No.83) Below *The Reapers*; by George Stubbs (No.84)

George Stubbs ARA (1724–1806)

Stubbs was a largely self-taught artist of strong and independent mind, whose purpose in travelling to Italy at the age of 21 (as many artists aspired to do in order to draw inspiration from antiquity and the Old Masters) was, as he put it, 'to convince himself that nature was and is always superior to art, Greek or Roman'. He satisfied his opinion and came home, beginning a rigorous course of anatomical study, shut away with the carcase of a horse in a Lincolnshire village, from which he published *The Anatomy of the Horse* in 1766. Stubbs's numerous paintings of horses and other animals are notable for their Neo-classical poise and composition, underpinned by his scientific knowledge. The *Reapers* and *Haymakers* are unusual in his work as country genre scenes, distinguished by their realism and their idealised compositions.

KITCHEN

In the 1930s, a large coal-fired black range stood in the middle of the parquet floor. Bill Smith, the son of the butler, recalled, 'When it was alight, which was most of the time, it felt like Hell's Kitchen – it was so hot.' This was the workplace of Lord Bearsted's Swiss chef, M. Dekker, who was known as a 'curmudgeon', and the four kitchen maids. M. Dekker's room was over the scullery, and his red face, with close-cropped hair and a bristly moustache, could survey the work going on below from an internal window. Mrs Jessie Clark, the cook at the Bearsteds' London house, also came down to Upton to share the workload.

According to Bill Smith, 'There were a couple of armchairs at the side of the range. Preparation of vegetables took place in the kitchen as well as in the scullery. There were wooden worktops. Washing was only done in the scullery. There was a cold room where puddings to be used again were kept. The larder was where the meat was kept.'

Servants' lives

Servants at Upton and other Bearsted houses enjoyed good conditions. In the 1930s, good domestic staff were rare, and it was worthwhile to treat them well. Bill Smith recalled, 'They organised a bus to take the women into Banbury shopping every Wednesday….The estate also ran a picture bus for a Wednesday after shopping which took anyone who wanted to one of the picture houses in Banbury.'

The servants ate well, and their meals were specially cooked for them, rather than being leftovers from the family. During the course of the year, various festivities could be expected, including presents at Christmas, although, being Jewish, the family did not keep the festival themselves.

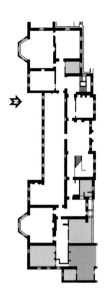

Below A menu card for a dinner held in June 1939 at the Bearsteds' London home

Food

Among English county families there was a long Victorian tradition that it was impolite to even mention the quality of food. This began to change as the reputation of French cooking spread, encouraged by the court of Edward VII and by international travel and luxury hotels. Surviving menus reveal that the Bearsteds' food was cooked in the finest French classical style. The supply of fresh produce from the kitchen gardens and hot houses at Upton, together with a general sense of liberality, would have made the meals here among the best of their time.

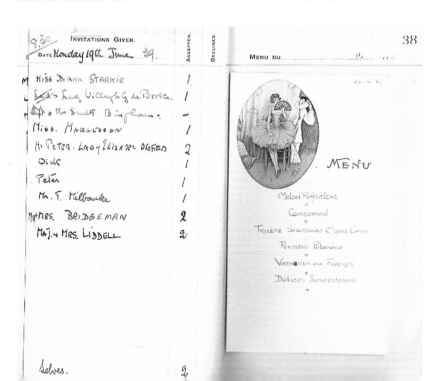

THE GARDENS

The Upton garden has a distinctive topography, with its steep terraces parallel to the house, and its combe-like water gardens lying to the side.

The bones of Sir Rushout Cullen's 17th-century garden remain legible in the main lawn and terracing, with the sequence of stewponds (where coarse fish were bred for the table) descending the valley from the neat brick Banqueting House that stands close to the source of water. Cullen's successor, William Bumstead, who lived at Upton between 1730 and 1757, probably planted the fine group of cedars of Lebanon. As the Trust's gardens adviser John Sales wrote of the next phase, 'It seems clear that the garden terraces and the whole valley garden were designed at least as much for use as for ornament. A plan of Robert Child's estate of 1774 indicates that full advantage was taken of the south-facing sloping plots below, for the production of fruit and vegetables. With fish from the ponds and nuts from the hazels, the garden must have fulfilled the early 18th-century ideal of abundant productivity. The garden retained this character into the 20th century. Only the upper terraces, clothed in evergreens, were adapted purely for pleasure.'

As found in 1927, the picturesque taste of the 19th century was only superficially applied, partly because little had been spent on bringing the garden up to date.

While the structure was good, the detailed planting had been neglected: glasshouses stood to the east of where the stone staircase now descends, and there was much for Lady Bearsted to work on, with her professional adviser, Kitty Lloyd Jones, and the Head Gardener, Mr Tidman.

A pioneering designer

Kathleen Lloyd Jones (1898–1978) was a pioneering English garden design consultant, who was educated on a course run by Kew Gardens in Regent's Park, and at Reading University. Upton came at the beginning of her career, and helped to establish her reputation as a meticulous planner of herbaceous borders, willing to spend many days instructing garden staff on the needs of different plants. She was a favourite with her clients, since she did not call for anything strikingly modern, and was happy to work with what already existed on the ground. As Rachel Berger writes in the Oxford *DNB*, 'Despite her demanding principles, her warmth and enthusiasm earned her affection from those who worked for her.' She also worked for Sir Felix and Lady Brunner at Greys Court, near Henley, and for Sir James Horlick on the island of Gigha in Argyllshire.

OPPOSITE

Top Tulips in an ornamental urn planter on the House Terrace

Far right Summer planting on the South Terrace

Right The Herbaceous Border and Mirror Pool in 1936

'Oh dear, the greenfly!'

'I have just made out a list of bulbs we should have for growing in pots and boxes for the house. I have taken into account suggestions you made last winter, e.g. more Sulphur Narcissus for London and more Hyacinths for really large bowls.

The garden will be looking very nice for this weekend I think. The Canterbury Bells are lovely and the roses quite good – but oh dear, the greenfly! It wants spraying nearly every day.'

Kitty Lloyd Jones to Lady Bearsted, June 1933

TOUR OF THE GARDENS

Numbers in this section refer to the map and key inside the front cover

1 NORTH DRIVE

Looking north from the forecourt, you can see that the line of the drive and the style of associated planting have remained the same as first recorded on the 1774 estate plan. A double avenue of mature Scots Pine with a collection of deciduous trees sits behind in an informal setting. Closer to the house, the avenue is interrupted with *Ilex aquifolium* and *Taxus baccata*.

2 FORECOURT

Apart from the shrub planting, this area still reflects the planting changes which were put in place by Kitty Lloyd Jones, with an interesting contrast of colours between the red-brick wall behind and the two green hues of the yew hedge and lawn in front.

Below Winter along the north driveway before arriving at the House

3 MAIN LAWN

4 House Terraces

Seasonal bedding displays of *Myosotis*, wall flowers and tulips in spring and Antirrhinums and Salvias in summer adorn the main terraces. To the east and west, dahlias, chrysanthemums and campanulas were used to extend the flowering period. Wisteria, clematis and climbing roses adorn the walls of the house. They make a stately contrast with the rich Hornton stonework behind.

5 Rock Garden

The Rock Garden sits on the east side of the lawn. Kitty Lloyd Jones conceived the original design and planting, using a selection of low but bold groups of rock plants that allow the rocks to feature prominently in the scheme.

6 Cedar Trees

The five Cedars of Lebanon were planted in the 18th century and adorn the landscape to the west of the garden. Over the years they have been cable-braced to retain their shape and structure.

Above Group of 5 magnificent Cedar Trees across the Main Lawn
Right Wisteria, forget-me-nots and tulips growing along the house borders

7 DRY BANKS

Beyond the lawn a sequence of three terraces runs west to east on the south-facing slope.

8 Top Terrace

Trained shrubs grow along the red-brick wall for spring interest: *Ceanothus*, roses and *Chaenomeles*. The border is adorned with foxtail and pineapple lilies, large groups of *Agapanthus* and interesting shrubby *Salvias* alongside the blue leaves and white flower heads of *Romneya*. The opposite border is planted with a double line of Lavender (*augustifolia*, 'Sawyers', 'Princess Purple' and 'Nana Alba'), which attracts nectar-loving insects.

Below The Middle Terrace border

9 Middle Terrace

A very dry hot south-facing terrace sits above the grass pathway, and showers of Mediterranean-type plants such as *Cistus*, *Brachyglottis* and *Ceanothus* are planted in repeated groups. *Nerine*, *Alliums* and species tulips are planted between. In the summer tender succulents add contrast to the groups.

Below the wall a continuous line of *Sisyrinchium striatum* follows the edge of the path.

'The north border facing the Laurel Bank, with the brick wall behind, would make an excellent border for late Michaelmas Daisies. Would you like to have this border for Michaelmas Daisies and Paeonies and the Irises (yellow) which are now in the little narrow border under the Laurel Bank? On the wall we could have Forsythias and other early spring shrubs which will do well on a north wall.'

Kitty Lloyd Jones, July 1931

10 Lower Terrace

To the west a steep bank of *Mahonia aquifolium* covers the ground, with tall Laburnum trees making informal silhouettes above. To the east, a graduated planting scheme of large shrubs through to smaller shrubs sits along the front of the border. A selection of *Berberis* plants grows well on the slope and provides interest throughout the year with early spring blossom, coloured berries and beautiful autumn shades of orange, yellow and red. Other groups of plants include *Olearia*, *Phlomis*, *Genista*, *Spartium* and *Cistus*. Kitty Lloyd Jones planted large irises in clumps through the border.

11 Autumn Border

This shady north-facing border was originally planted by Kitty Lloyd Jones with Michaelmas daisies and yellow flag irises and was quite spectacular in late spring. Today, a fine collection of late flowering herbaceous plants can be found including different cultivars of Aster, *Symphyotrichum* and *Chrysanthemum*. It is a sight not to be missed in late September.

12 Scented Garden

Before you depart the terraces, poke your head through the archway in the wall and smell the perfumes coming from the Scented Garden. This area was used for growing-on plants. To the south is the wild garden – an oasis of spring bulbs and winter-flowering trees.

Right *Osteospermum jucundum* (African daisy)

Left Autumn border

Above Courgettes in the Kitchen Garden

Below Lupins in flower in the North Lake Border

13 THE MIDDLE SECTION

14 The Herbaceous Borders
Designed by Kitty Lloyd Jones.

A set of double borders runs south for 60 metres and is reflected in the Mirror Pool beyond. The borders come alive in the middle of July with their bold reflective planting groups, shocking pinks and bright yellow flowers, forever repeating themselves along the length of the borders adding a touch of seasonal colour and structure.

15 North Lake Border
Designed by Kitty Lloyd Jones.

This early summer border comes into flower towards the end of May and is a magnificent display of early herbaceous plants. *Delphinium*, Lupin and Iris are the backbone to the border whilst other plants infill and drift through the gaps to make a stunning show of colour. This border was described as 'a high bank of colour' in a 1930s *Country Life* article and it will be so once again.

'At the moment the lake border is 3 or 4 feet deep in weed taken out of the lake. It took all the men nearly a week to weed it and it's not really clean yet. But I hope it will be really clean before bathing next year.'

Kitty Lloyd Jones, 9 August 1932

16 The Mirror Pool and South Lake Border
Behind you is the Mirror Pool, in which are reflected the nearby borders and pasture lands. The pool is home to red-finned Rudd, which flash about in grand style. The border opposite has groups of shade-tolerant plants which like a slightly heavier, damper soil. Walk along and smell the *Clematis* 'Wyevale' and hear the rattling stems of the *Miscanthus × gigantea* rustle in the breeze. From the corner look back to see the chimneypots on the house.

17 Kitchen Garden

This part of the garden has remained in productive cultivation since the house was built. In 1774 the plan shows the south slope divided into twelve plots stretching west from the east wall to the hedge, running north to the red-brick wall and as far south as the Mirror Pool.

Today, the plot is somewhat smaller, but it is quite unusual for a kitchen garden to be the focal point of a garden. Needless to say, it is still very productive and offers handy lessons on growing seasonal fruit and seed for next year's crops. The upper slope grows a vast assortment of vegetables from asparagus to sweet corn, and the lower slope is home to a collection of different types of trained soft fruit. Look out for Upton delicacies on the menu in the Pavilion restaurant.

18 Delphinium Border

The border is planted as a blue border with *Delphiniums*. Blue *Delphiniums*, *Geraniums* and late flowering shrubby *Caryopteris* provide a backdrop to the trained stoned fruit trees of apricot, peach and nectarine on the south facing wall.

Above Looking back to the Kitchen Garden from the Mirror Pool

Admirable Asters and Symphyotrichum

Upton has looked after the National Collection of asters since 1985. Several species and cultivars are grown to show the many different plants in the aster group and to make a spectacular display. The collection is at its best in September.

19 THE FORMAL GARDENS

20 Rose Garden

Designed by Kitty Lloyd Jones.

The Rose Garden sits in a quiet corner behind a large yew hedge just west of the fruit garden. The garden is planted with opposite beds of pinks and China roses of the kind available in the 1930s and flowers for a lengthy period. A statue of Pan sits in the middle.

21 Lady Bearsted's Garden

Designed by Kitty Lloyd Jones.

The 1904 plan shows two glasshouses on this site, which possibly grew early varieties of salad and vegetables. These were removed by the 1930s, and a garden was designed for Lady Bearsted. The colour scheme was pale pinks and white with flowering shrubs, herbaceous plants and seasonal bedding. Tulips and early spring bedding plants are now used to extend the seasonal display.

22 Hibiscus Garden

Designed by Tony Lord, former National Trust gardens adviser for Upton.

This area was probably used for growing-on hardy stock plants. The current scheme of *Hibiscus*, *Eryngium* and early bulbs followed by later-flowering dark purple tulips was designed in 1984.

Right The statue of Pan, Greek god of woods and fields, in the Rose Garden

Opposite Lady Bearsted's Garden in the spring

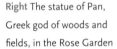

Gardener's tip

Adding mulch to your borders not only improves their appearance, but also helps suppress annual weed growth, retains moisture levels, and improves the soil structure.

23 WEST GARDEN

24 Sunken Lawn

This area was once one of a sequence of medieval stewponds. In 1955 it was planted with a group of cherry trees, but the area flooded, and the middle section of trees died, leaving the outer ring, which was later felled when it became infected with canker.

Today, the borders contain an interesting group of ferns to the south and a collection of *Hemerocallis* to the west. Soft fruit are trained against the red-brick walls, which are laid in a pattern known as 'Flemish Bond'.

25 The Stewpond

It sits between the Sunken Garden and the Bog Garden and is home to a collection of ornamental carp.

26 Bog Garden

Designed by Kitty Lloyd Jones.

This was also formerly a stewpond. A freshwater spring runs into the north-west corner of the garden to feed the water features. The water rills, falls and pools were put in place in the late 1930s, and a sequence of beds was created to grow a very different selection of plants from those in the very dry borders on the terraces to the east.

The lower beds house large drifts of moisture-loving plants such as *Rodgersia*, *Ligularia* and the dominating giant-leaved *Gunnera*. At the further extremities there are collections of shrubs and shade-tolerant herbaceous plants.

A continuous planting programme is in progress to develop the planting groups. In the spring you can see things growing overnight in this magical area.

Right The Bog Garden in summer

Gardener's view

The plants in the Bog Garden explode into life in mid-May and turn this area into a green oasis, casting light and shadows into every corner. Watch the *Osmunda regalis* (Royal Fern) unwind its fronds by the monks' well.

27 Yew Terraces

They consist of three different interlocking terraces which eventually wind their way back up to the house. The 1774 plan shows clipped yews planted in pairs along the terraces. The terraces remained unaltered until the 1970s, when a programme of planting was put in hand to replace fallen trees. The bark on the mature yew trees has a wonderful marble effect.

A pleasant walk takes you back to the main lawn, with views across to Bog Cottage, a late 17th-century banqueting house that nestles in the boundary wall. Prolong your stay by booking the cottage for a holiday and watch the wildlife from your breakfast table.

28 ORCHARD

Designed by Kitty Lloyd Jones.

The last port of call takes you through the orchard by the east side of the house. The orchard was laid out in 1932, when many cultivars of apples and pears were planted on a grid system. Drifts of *Narcissus* lined the pathways in the spring.

Today, the orchard also includes greengages, plums, medlars and mulberry trees. Early 1930 varieties of *Narcissus* can be found growing along the pathways in early spring to lead you to much-needed refreshments in the Pavilion restaurant.

Above The late 17th-century Banqueting House (now Bog Cottage)

EARLY HISTORY

Upton is a property that has changed hands many times. During the reign of Richard I, at the end of the 12th century, it was held by the Arden family, who granted part of the land to the canons of St Sepulchre's in Warwick. The first record of a family with the name of de Upton comes in 1200, but in the following century the estate passed to the Verneys of Wolford, near Shipston-on-Stour. It seems to have been styled a manor for the first time in 1452, when William, son of Robert Verney, sold it to Richard Dalby, from whom it passed to Sir William Danvers at the end of the 15th century. During the next 20 years, it seems likely that a house was built, of which some fabric remains in the basement of the present house. Several generations later in the same family, John Danvers was the owner at the time of the Battle of Edgehill in 1642 which took place a mile away near Radway. The Archers of Tysoe succeeded the Danverses, when their line died out.

The builder of the house

Upton was sold to Sir Rushout Cullen, Bt, some time before 1695, the date that appears on the rainwater heads with his initials. The son of a city merchant, Cullen created the central nine bays. (The single-storey wings, which form the lower levels of the bay windows flanking the south front, were added in the 18th century.)

Perhaps the most striking element of the building is the Hornton stone, with its rich textured honey-brown colour. The quarry is off the Banbury–Stratford road close to Upton, though no longer in use.

Above Plan of the Upton estate in 1774, when it was owned by the Child family

William Bumstead

Cullen had no children, and on his death the house was sold to William Bumstead, who is chiefly remembered for his acrimonious correspondence with his neighbour, Sanderson Miller, the gentleman-architect who built the Radway tower (now the Castle Inn) to commemorate the centenary of Edgehill. Bumstead was probably responsible for aggrandising the house with the broken segmental (shallow curved) pediment on the north front, and the doorcase of Clipsham stone below it. Rainwater heads dated 1735 are found on this side of the house, giving a probable date for the work. While segmental gables and doorcases were frequently used by Italian Baroque architects and their English followers, the form seen at Upton, with a section cut away in the centre, is more often found in furniture (especially longcase clocks) than in buildings. This suggests that it was the work of a local master mason rather than a fashionable architect.

Touched by scandal

In 1757 Bumstead sold Upton to Francis Child, head of one of the major banking dynasties of the time and the patron of Robert Adam at Osterley Park in Middlesex. Architecturally, Upton remained largely untouched. In 1804 Francis Child's grand-niece, Lady Sarah Sophia Fane, married the 5th Earl of Jersey, bringing Upton as part of her extensive dowry. The Child inheritance skipped a generation, as Lady Sarah's mother had eloped dramatically in 1782 with the impoverished 10th Earl of Westmorland, marrying under Scottish law after a dash to Gretna Green – the angry father in pursuit! He would have caught them had the Earl not shot his leading horse dead on the road.

Ignored by fashion

History and fashion continued to pass Upton by, and it remained a minor residence, empty or let to tenants of the Earls of Jersey, who had a larger house at Middleton Stoney in north Oxfordshire. In 1894 Upton was sold to Mr Andrew Motion, the grandfather and namesake of the former Poet Laureate. The rather conventionally furnished interiors of this time, with Jacobean-style plaster decoration on some of the ceilings, were recorded in photographs by *Country Life*, when it featured the house in 1904.

Below This winter view of Upton from the south was painted by Arthur Devis about 1803. It shows the temple at the opposite end of the lake from its present position

SAMUEL FAMILY TREE

Marcus Samuel, 1st Viscount Bearsted = Fanny Benjamin
(1853–1927) | (1858–1927)
m.1881

Walter, 2nd Viscount Bearsted = Dorothea Micholls
(1885–1948) | (1885–1949)

Marcus Richard (Dick) = (1) Heather Firmston Williams
3rd Viscount Bearsted | (1926–93)
(1909–86) | m.1947, div.1966

(2) Jean Agnew
(d.1978)
m.1968

Peter, = (1) Deirdre du Barry de Lavey
4th Viscount | m.1939, div.1942
Bearsted
(1911–96) | (2) Elizabeth Cohen
(d.1983)
m.1946

(3) Nina Hilary
m.1984

Daphne | Anthony
(1913–14) | (1917–2001)

Nicholas Alan
5th Viscount Samuel
(b.1950)

Below A hunt meet in the forecourt at Upton